JOSHUA
in the Promised Land

JOSHUA
in the Promised Land

BY MIRIAM CHAIKIN

Woodcuts by David Frampton

CLARION BOOKS
NEW YORK

Thanks are due to Rabbi M. Walter Neumann
for reading and commenting on the manuscript.

Clarion Books
a Houghton Mifflin Company imprint
215 Park Avenue South, New York, NY 10003
Text copyright © 1982 by Miriam Chaikin
Woodcuts copyright © 1982 by David Frampton
All rights reserved.
For information about permission to reproduce
selections from this book, write to Permissions,
Houghton Mifflin Company, 215 Park Avenue South, New York, NY 10003.
Printed in the USA

Library of Congress Cataloging in Publication Data
Chaikin, Miriam.   Joshua in the Promised Land.
Summary: Retells the biblical story of Joshua who, in
succeeding Moses as the leader of the Israelites,
masterminded the conquest of Canaan, the Promised Land.
1. Joshua, son of Nun—Juvenile literature.
2. Bible. O.T.—Biography—Juvenile.
[1. Joshua, son of Nun. 2. Bible stories—O.T.]
I. Frampton, David, ill. II. Title.
BS580.J7C45   222'.20924   [B]   82-4131
ISBN 0-89919-120-7   PA ISBN 0-395-54797-0   AACR2

VB   10   9   8   7   6

For Selma Wrubel Elkes
and in memory of Irwin Elkes
and for Peggy Mann, W. W.

CONTENTS

FOREWORD

Little is known of Joshua. The Hebrew Bible, also called the Old Testament, tells us only that he was the son of Nun of the tribe of Ephraim. It tells us nothing about his mother, not even her name. From the same source we know that Joshua left Egypt with Moses when that great leader freed the Israelites from slavery and marched with them toward the Promised Land. In a sentence or two, we learn that Moses chose Joshua over his own sons to lead the Israelites in battle and that Joshua accompanied him to Mount Sinai when he went up to receive the Law, and waited for him below.

Beyond this, we know nothing of the man. Yet his qualities were such that over thousands of others he was chosen to succeed Moses and to bring the Israelites into the Promised Land.

Joshua in the Promised Land is a faithful retelling of the episodes that make up the biblical account. The ancient Israelites are commanded by God to conquer Canaan (ancient Israel). At the time, the land is inhabited by pagan nations who worship idols and burn their own children in sacrifices. Their form of worship involves other hideous practices as well. God's command to Joshua has two parts.

He tells Joshua and the Israelites to go in and fight for the land He has promised to give them. He also charges them with the responsibility to destroy the pagans and their idols and altars and to install in the land the worship of God.

I have condensed an episode or two in the retelling. And I have added fictional elements to the basic account, inventing for Joshua a household with wife, young son and daughter, maidservant and manservant, ascribing thoughts and motivations to him, and creating dialogue for each scene. The story is now played out against the background of the everyday life of the times.

M.C.

JOSHUA
in the Promised Land

INTRODUCTION

More than three thousand years ago, in the thirteenth century B.C.E. (Before the Common Era), the Pharaoh Rameses II ruled Egypt. Wishing to be known as a great builder, Rameses called for new cities to be built in Egypt. For labor, he enslaved the Israelites to toil for him.

The Israelites were the descendants of Jacob of Canaan, a land east of Egypt, and his wives. About four hundred years before, a famine had overtaken Canaan. Jacob had led all his people, with all their possessions, to Egypt, where food was plentiful. His son Joseph was a powerful minister to the Egyptian king. Years later, when Jacob died, he was given a royal funeral in Egypt. But his body was buried in Canaan.

For centuries, the Israelites prospered in Egypt. But at the time of Rameses II, they had become slaves. And they toiled without end in the blazing sun while harsh slavemasters stood over them and prodded them to make yet another brick, then another.

The wretched Israelites cried out in pain. They begged God to help them. God heard their pleas and chose Moses to save them. One day, as Moses went with his flock from Midian to the Sinai wilderness to search for grazing land, the voice of God came to him and told him to go to Egypt and free the Israelites and bring them to the Promised Land.

Moses was reluctant to go. He was a stammerer and slow of speech. "Who am I that I should go to Pharaoh and bring the Israelites out of Egypt?" he said.

But God insisted. God told Moses to set out on the journey and to take his brother Aaron to speak for him. And God gave Moses miracles to use. These were to prove to the Israelites and to the Pharaoh that Moses had been sent by God.

Moses and Aaron set out for Egypt. With Aaron acting as spokesman, Moses pleaded with the Pharaoh to let the Israelites go. But the Pharaoh refused. He needed slaves to make bricks for his cities.

Since pleading failed, Moses made use of the miracles. He turned the waters of the Nile River into blood, causing the fish to perish. He made frogs and lice appear, and affliction to follow affliction, until the Pharaoh was forced to relent.

"Go, and take your people with you," the Pharaoh said.

In the year 1230 B.C.E., the Israelites left Egypt. Moses, then eighty years old, led them out into the wilderness toward Canaan, where their ancestor Jacob was buried. Canaan was the land that God had given the Israelites to inherit.

Now, "to inherit the land" meant to conquer it, for the land was inhabited. But Moses saw almost at once that the people were not up to the task. They were numerous enough. There were twelve tribes, each springing from one of the twelve sons of Jacob. But they were like so many children. They had been slaves too long. Endless labor in the blazing sun and a lack of education had made them foolish. They chased after trinkets, thought only of their stomachs, and fell easily into idol worship. Such a people could not be counted on to conquer a land.

To gain time, Moses wandered slowly toward the Promised Land, of which he knew nothing. In the second year, as the Israelites drew near the southern border of the land, he called together twelve men, one from each tribe, and sent them in to spy out the land. Among the twelve were Joshua of the tribe of Ephraim and Caleb of the tribe of Judah.

When the spies returned, ten said Canaan was occupied by giants and that the Israelites would be slain if they went in. Joshua and Caleb said there was nothing to fear.

"It is a great and good land, a land of milk and honey," Joshua said.

"Behold its riches," Caleb said, showing the fruit he had brought back: pomegranates, figs, and grapes that were larger than dates.

The people ignored the words of Joshua and Caleb and refused to go in. They had been frightened by the dark tales. There was nothing for Moses to do but to take them wandering again. He needed much more time to make a nation of them. They had to be trained in courage and taught about God.

Moses wandered with them for a total of forty years, encamping now at an oasis, now wandering on again. At the end of that time he had molded them into a new nation. The slaves had all died. Of those who had left Egypt, only Moses, Joshua, and Caleb were still alive. Every other person— every tribe member and the head of every tribe—had been

born in the desert and was free. Moses had taught the Law.
Joshua had taught warfare. Aaron had become high priest
and died. His son Eleazar, the new high priest, led the people in the worship of God.

Now that the Israelites had become a nation and a new
race, Moses deemed them ready to enter Canaan. He
brought them to Shittim, on the plains of Moab, along the

eastern bank of the Jordan River. This was land that the Israelites had won by defeating two Moabite kings, Sihon of Heshbon and Og of Bashan.

Here the Israelites camped for the last time outside of Canaan. They set up the Tabernacle, their tent of worship, as they had done at each encampment during their wandering. And within they put the ark containing the Holy Law that God had commanded them to obey. In front of the Tabernacle, in the center of a large courtyard, they set up the altar of sacrifice on a hill.

This was the Tabernacle compound. Around it, in a square, the Israelites pitched their black tents of goatskin, so that three tribes dwelled on each side. The tents of the seventy elders faced the Tabernacle compound. Behind them were the tents of their clansmen. Moses' tent was at the edge of the courtyard, opposite the entrance to the Tabernacle.

Moses stood gazing about at the new surroundings. The river Jordan was a short march away. On the other side of it was Canaan. The Israelites stood on the threshold of the Promised Land and were about to enter it. But Moses was not to be among them. He knew that, because God had told him so. Even so, he yearned to set foot on the land toward which he had been wandering for so long. He wondered: Could he perhaps persuade God to relent? He crossed the courtyard and went into the Tabernacle to plead.

But God was adamant. "You are old and stricken in years, and you shall not enter the land," God said. "Go to the top of Mount Nebo and see it from there. But send Joshua in to possess the land."

God went on speaking, giving Moses yet other commands, and Moses remained and listened. Some of the commands were for him to obey; others were intended for Joshua.

Disappointed, Moses left the Tabernacle. He paused in the courtyard to glance up at the sky. The first days of spring brought changeable weather. A rain had fallen earlier, cooling off the earth. But now a bright sun shone overhead.

Moses draped his robe over his left arm and walked wearily toward Joshua's tent.

·1·

JOSHUA

The ashes in the cooking pit outside Joshua's tent were still warm. Channa, the maidservant, had just prepared a meal over the fire. The heat of day made eating outside unpleasant. But it was comfortable inside the tent. The goatskin of which the tent was made kept out the sun, and the open flaps let the dry winds of the east rush through.

Joshua sat at the back of the tent with Pnina, his wife. Their grown children were married and lived in tents of their own. With them were their two youngest children, Jochebed, a little girl of eight, named for Moses' mother, and Amram, a boy of ten, named for Moses' father.

Before them, on the ground, was a large bowl of lentils and onions that Channa had cooked. Channa and Carmi, the manservant, sat with the family, scooping up lentils in the folds of a flat bread.

"Who walks in the heat of day?" Joshua asked, noticing a figure approaching outside. He leaped to his feet when he saw who it was.

"*Adoni!* Master!" he said, as Moses entered.

"*Moshe rabbenu!* Moses, our teacher!" the children cried.

Moses nodded to them and told Joshua he wished to speak with him.

"Lower the curtain, Carmi," Joshua called.

As the manservant dropped a curtain from the top, shutting off the rear and dividing the tent into two rooms, Joshua wondered why Moses had come. He usually left his tent only to go to the morning and evening sacrifices. Certainly he never went out in the heat of day.

The manservant arranged a woven blanket on the floor and pillows to lean against, then left a bowl of fruit and withdrew behind the curtain.

Joshua and Moses seated themselves. Joshua broke open a pomegranate and chewed the juice of its seeds as he waited for Moses to compose his speech.

"I have this day spoken to God and received commands for you," Moses said a moment later. "Also for myself," he added. "I am not to enter the land. I am old and stricken in years. God told me: 'Send Joshua in to possess the land.' "

Joshua could not conceal his surprise. God had chosen Moses and spoken to him face to face. Why should Moses not enter the land? Gently, so as to give no offense, he framed the question.

Color rose in the pale cheeks, under a beard that was yellow with age. Moses' lips grappled with speech. "I-I angered God in the d-desert," he said. "You will recall when the people complained of thirst and I struck a stone?"

Joshua nodded.

"God had told me to strike the stone. And when water came forth, I let it seem as if it were my doing and not the work of God."

Joshua looked away. The confession embarrassed him.

He had never seen this great man in an ordinary light before. "And the other commands?" he said.

Moses' lips struggled to tame his speech. "The land of Canaan is inhabited by seven wicked nations," he said. "They pray to idols—to Astarte, a fertility goddess, and Baal, a rainmaker god. And they burn their children in sacrifice to these idols. God commands you to drive wickedness out of the land by destroying these nations, and their idols and altars along with them. Leave their cities a heap and a rubble.''

"All that God commands will I do," Joshua said.

"Further, you are commanded to take a census of our people and to lead the nation into Canaan on the first day of the month of Nisan.''

Joshua looked up. He had heard all that Moses had said. But only now did he grasp the situation. Moses had led the people up to the Promised Land. But it would be left to him, Joshua, to bring them in and to fight for the land.

"The people will surely follow me in combat, as they have before, but will they accept me as their leader?" he asked.

Moses placed a hand on Joshua's arm. "They know that I have chosen you over my own sons," Moses replied. "They know that you accompanied me to Mount Sinai when I went up to receive the Law, and waited for me below. They know you slew King Og and King Sihon in battle and inherited this land of Moab on which we are now encamped. Be strong and of good courage, and God will not fail you.''

·2·

TWO AND A HALF TRIBES

Eleazar, the high priest, suddenly stood in the door of the tent.

"Welcome, enter," Joshua said.

Eleazar entered and bowed before Moses. "*Adoni,* master," he said. "The elders of Reuben, Gad, and half of Manasseh wish to have an audience with you."

"What has arisen?" Moses asked.

Eleazar pointed outside. "It is about these grassy lands of Moab," he said. "The land is good for cattle, and they wish to remain here with their herds."

Joshua was not surprised to see Moses' lips twitching with anger. "R-r-remain here, east of the Jordan, and n-n-not cross over into Canaan with the others?" Moses said.

Eleazar shrugged. "That is what they say, master."

"G-gather the elders in the Tent of Meeting," Moses said. "We will join you there."

Eleazar bowed and left.

Joshua was himself vexed. It would rob him of warriors if two and a half tribes stayed behind. He had much to think about. But not now. Moses had extended his arm and was ready to leave. Joshua got up, took his arm, and helped him to rise.

"A moment, *adoni,*" Joshua said, and went behind the curtain. He spoke a few words to his wife, then followed Moses out.

Joshua gathered his robe over his left arm, and both men walked along the row of tents that faced the courtyard, toward Moses' tent. In the heat of day, few people were about. Two women walked with pitchers toward the well. They bowed as they passed. Some children rushing to fill their empty goatskins with water paused before Moses, said "*Adoni,*" and ran on.

Joshua smiled to himself when he saw his son running

with an unlit torch toward the fire well. The boy had lost no time in leaving the tent. He was running to get fire, but not for his mother. He had taken a liking to a girl from the tribe of Benjamin. The fire was for her mother.

They arrived at Moses' tent and went in. A great sadness came over Joshua as he glanced about at Moses' possessions: the heavy, sleeved coat that he wore in the cold and also slept on, folded on the floor; a small oil lamp next to it; and all around, piles of clay tablets on which Moses wrote the story of the Israelites. Joshua shuddered as he realized that he might never again see his beloved master moving among the familiar furnishings of this tent.

"Behold," Moses said, standing over a carrying case made of goatskin. "Inside are the bones of Joseph, which I brought out of Egypt with me."

Joshua drew closer. He was descended from Ephraim, the son of Joseph. He touched the carrying case, feeling a kinship.

"Jacob, his father," Moses continued, "bought a parcel of land in Shechem for a hundred pieces of money. When the land is yours bury Joseph there in Canaan. It was his wish."

"It shall be done," Joshua said.

Moses tapped a tablet with his finger. "From Jacob and both his wives, Leah and Rachel, are all the twelve tribes descended," he said. "The story is written here. Speak of it to the people so that they do not forget."

Joshua smiled. Moses had said that to him many times. "You have taught them well, *adoni*, and they know about our ancestors. But I shall continue to speak of them," he answered.

Joshua felt burdened as he walked to the outskirts of the camp, toward the Tent of Meeting. *When the land is yours*, Moses had said. Again the question of preparedness arose. He had warriors enough to battle against the marauding tribes of the desert here in Moab. But did he have enough to take the land across the Jordan, with its walled cities?

"*Adoni*," he said. "The wicked nations are seven, and they are mighty. Does Israel have enough warriors to take the land?"

"When you have taken the census, you will know," Moses said. He glanced at Joshua from the corner of his eye. "Only believe in God, and all will go well with you," he added.

·3·

THE TENT OF MEETING

Seated on goatskins and blankets on the floor of the Tent of Meeting were the people that Eleazar had assembled—the elders and nobles of the tribes of Simeon, Judah, Issachar, Ephraim, Zebulon, Benjamin, Dan, Asher, Naphtali, and the half of the tribe of Manasseh that was descended from Joseph. Sitting off to a side were the two and a half tribes that wished to remain behind—Reuben, Gad, and the other half of Manasseh. Caleb, Eleazar, the high priest, and other priests, the chief scribe, and others sat among them.

It grew still as Moses entered. Joshua walked with Moses

to the rear of the tent, where they seated themselves, Moses in the center and Joshua to the side.

Moses began to speak. "Now that we are ready to enter the land, two and a half tribes have expressed a desire to stay here," he said. "The people of Reuben, Gad, and half of Manasseh wish to remain on this side of the Jordan."

"Here?" people asked in surprise. "On *this* side of the Jordan?"

Moses turned toward the tribes. "Speak, and let us hear what you have to say."

A woman from the tribe of Reuben arose, dark eyes alert in an ancient face. *"Adoni,"* she said. "Our hearts yearn to go with the others to the Promised Land. But we are herds-people and need food for our cattle. Metalsmiths, carpenters, and weavers may go anywhere. Shepherds, too, for sheep eat little and goats find food enough between the stones. But cattle eat a great deal."

She turned to the other tribes. "Many of our cattle died in the parched lands of our wandering," she said. "We do not know what land lies on the other side of the Jordan. We know only that this land is grassy and good for cattle. For this reason alone do we wish to remain here."

Moses looked away. *Again, a few people concerned only for themselves and not for the nation as a whole,* he thought. *Will it never end?*

Joshua waited to hear how Moses would reply.

Moses composed himself, then began to speak. "You c-c-can't remain here while others cross over to fight for the land," he said. "But I will make a covenant with you," he added. "If the women and children remain here with the herds, and the men cross over to fight with the others, I will give you this land when the fighting is over."

Joshua smiled to himself. Moses had saved his army for him.

The woman sat to speak with her people, then rose again.

"We accept, *adoni*," she said.

Moses glanced first at Joshua, then at the others. "You, Joshua, and all of you assembled here have witnessed my vow," he said. "Fulfill it when the land is won. Fulfill also this vow." His eyes rested for an instant on Caleb. "For serving God all the days of his life, Caleb shall receive land of his own, for himself and his clan."

Caleb bowed his head.

"It shall be done," Joshua said as the elders repeated the words with him.

"I have this day spoken to God," Moses then said. "This evening, after the sacrifice, I shall repeat God's words for you." He folded his hands in his lap, a sign that he had finished speaking.

"Delay yourself a moment, Eleazar," he called as everyone rose to leave.

Joshua went to stand beside Moses as Eleazar approached.

"After the sacrifice," Moses said to Eleazar, "I shall name Joshua my successor. Prepare oil for the anointment."

Eleazar bowed to Moses, then to Joshua, and left.

Moses extended his arm, and Joshua helped him to rise.

"Adoni," Joshua said. "Your decision was a good one. With one stroke, you gave them what they asked and also preserved my army."

Moses smiled. "You will need a strong fighting army," he said. "Come, take me home. I want to rest."

Joshua walked alongside Moses. Clouds had appeared in the sky, turning the air cool, and many people now sat outside their tents.

Joshua paused at Moses' tent. "When you have taken the census, bring the numbers to me so that I might write them on my tablets," Moses said.

·4·
A CENSUS IS TAKEN

Joshua's grown sons and daughters and those of other elders and nobles divided themselves into groups and went throughout the camp. Coming before the head of each tribe, they asked how many souls there were in that tribe, and of these, how many were mighty men of valor and the best warriors. They asked how many were too young to fight, and how many too old, and also took a count of the women, children, and infants of all ages.

The census gatherers brought the numbers to Joshua in his tent. As he received them, he etched them in wet clay, and when he added them together, he felt a great rush of joy. He saw God's wisdom in the command to take a census. For he now knew that he had a mighty army for hand-to-hand combat and hundreds more who were not yet fully trained, if he needed them. The task he had been charged with suddenly seemed possible, and he had nothing to fear.

His heart swelled with joy. He went to the door of the tent and looked across the courtyard. Smoke rose from the perpetually burning altar. He yearned to seek the presence of the Lord in the Tabernacle. But first, the numbers. Moses was waiting for them. He gathered up the tablets and brought them to his master, then walked across the courtyard to the Tabernacle.

He rejoiced as he drew near and thought back to the time that it was built. He was only a small boy then. But his parents often spoke of it. God had commanded Moses to build a Tabernacle, saying, "Make me a sanctuary, that I may dwell among you." God had named the exact materials that were to be used and given exact measurements for the size. Moses told it all to Bezalel of the tribe of Judah, the chief builder. Bezalel, with his helpers, began to build the Tabernacle.

They made a frame of acacia wood on sockets of silver. And as a covering over it all, they used first fine twined linen, then goatskins, then rams' skins dyed red and, on top, dolphin skins.

The Tabernacle was holy. Joshua could not go in without purifying himself first. He washed his hands and feet in the brass laver that stood near the embroidered screen door, then went in.

The air of the first chamber was still heavy with the scent of frankincense that Eleazar had burned during the morning sacrifice. Joshua paused before the curtain of gold thread that led to the second chamber. Behind the curtain, in the second chamber, was the holy of holies. This chamber

housed the ark that held the Law that God had given Moses on Mount Sinai, two tables of stone, written on both sides.

Trembling before the holy chamber, Joshua lifted the curtain and went in. Before him was the ark made of acacia wood. On top of it, guarding the law, were two cherubim of hammered gold with outstretched wings. The presence of God came sometimes to rest between their wings.

Joshua stood with bowed head before the ark.

"Holy, holy God, creator of all that is and ever was and ever will be, Master of the universe," he said, stretching out his arms toward the space between the wings. Then, over-flowing with love and rapture, he fell on his face and spoke what was in his heart.

·5·

JOSHUA IS ANOINTED

Joshua emerged from the Tabernacle refreshed and se-rene. He saw that people were beginning to gather for the evening sacrifice, and hurried to his tent.

Pnina sat combing Jochebed's hair.

"Father," Jochebed said. "The children say that you are to be our new leader."

"Then you must obey me," Joshua said. He kissed Jo-chebed, then hurried behind the curtain to cleanse himself with oil and put on a fresh robe. As he dressed, he could hear the sound of the high priest's bells. They hung on the hem of his robe and jingled as he walked. It was a signal that he had arrived at the Tabernacle compound.

"There are Eleazar's bells," Jochebed called.

"Yes, and I must hurry," Joshua said. He oiled his hair and beard and came out from behind the curtain.

"Where is Amram?" he asked.

"I don't know," Pnina said. "I have sent Carmi to the

tents of Benjamin to look for him." She went with Joshua to the door of the tent. "Go. We will come later," she said.

Joshua folded his robe over his left arm and went out. He made his way through the crowd to the altar of sacrifice in the Tabernacle courtyard. Moses and Eleazar had already ascended the hill of the altar. Joshua hurried up the hill.

Behind Eleazar, on a table, were a slaughtered lamb and a cup of its blood. Eleazar raised an arm to silence the crowd, then turned to the lamb. He placed one hand on its head and with the other hand sprinkled blood about the altar. The altar priests then carried the lamb to the mesh grill on the four horns of the altar and placed it on the flame.

Turning to face the people, Eleazar closed his eyes and stretched his arms heavenward. "Great and good God, Creator of all life, Master of the seas, Hewer of mountains, Keeper of the moons, Source of all that is, Thee and Thee alone do we worship and to Thine honor and glory do we offer up this lamb."

"Holy, holy, holy is God," Moses and Joshua said.

"Holy are all the works of God," the people answered.

Joshua then commanded the trumpet blowers in the courtyard below to sound the call of general assembly. They lifted up their trumpets of beaten silver and blew, first one, then the other. At the sound, whoever had stayed behind came out of the tents to listen.

Moses stepped to the front of the altar and raised his arms. "Hear, O Israel, we have but one God and one God alone," he said. His eye was keen, his voice firm. Only the sunken cheeks beneath the yellowing beard betrayed his age. "Praise God, serve Him in joy, come before Him in jubilation. Know that the Lord is God. He made us, and we are His.''

"God was, God is, God will ever be,'' Joshua and the people answered.

"You are about to enter the land that God has given you to inherit,'' Moses said. "This day has God spoken to me and commanded me to send Joshua in to possess the land. Follow him and obey him in all things.''

"As we are with you, so shall we be with Joshua,'' the people answered.

Joshua fixed his gaze on the flaming colors in the sky to keep from crying. The people did not yet understand that Moses would soon not be with them, that he would soon be dead. Seeing Eleazar approach with the oil, Joshua bent his head.

As Eleazar poured oil on his head, Moses placed a hand on Joshua's shoulder. In that moment, the presence of God, in the form of a pillar of cloud, passed by the Tabernacle door.

"May God bless you and keep you,'' Moses said. "May God deal kindly and graciously with you. May God favor you and be your friend.''

"Amen,'' the people answered with one voice.

"Israelites,'' Moses said, "love your God with all your heart and all your soul and all your might. Remember those words. Teach them to your children. Speak of them at all times, when you lie down, when you rise up, in your home, and out.''

Joshua raised his head. He could not take his eyes from Moses. The glory of God was upon him, and he shone.

"You are going to a good land," Moses continued, "a land of brooks and springs, of wheat and barley, of vines and fig trees and pomegranates, a land of milk and honey."

In the silence, the flames could be heard consuming the lamb.

"On the fourteenth day of Nisan, at God's command, your parents kept the Passover in Egypt, where they had been slaves. You are now a free nation. Celebrate your freedom on the fourteenth day after you arrive in the land of your inheritance. Celebrate it then and for all time."

The sun sank, taking with it the colors that had lit up the sky.

"Keep the Law that God has given you, and all will go well with you in the land," Moses said as darkness spread across the sky.

·6·

MOSES DIES

Moses went up to the top of Mount Nebo, as the Lord had commanded, and beheld the Promised Land. He saw below him the waters of the Jordan, the rich green fields of Jericho, and beyond, the hills of Jerusalem. In the north he saw the snowcapped mountains of Lebanon and in the south, the edge of the desert. It was, as he had told the people, a land of milk and honey. Moses went down from the mountain.

He had seen the land, as God had commanded, and died without entering it, as God had decreed.

On Saturday, as the day began to cool, shouts rang throughout the camp. "The servant of God is no more! Moses is dead!" People beat their breasts and wept when they heard the news.

Joshua tore his robe in mourning and sprinkled ashes on

his head. He fell on the ground and wept. No more would he gaze upon the beloved face of his master.

Later, when he and the others had composed themselves, Joshua brought up the subject of burial. All were agreed that Moses should be buried in a secret place. He had been touched by God and was holy. Not Abraham, not Isaac, not Jacob, but Moses alone had seen the face of God. If his burial place were known, the ignorant and curious were certain to seek it out, to look upon the holy face.

In the night, under cover of darkness, Joshua, Caleb, and their sons went from the camp with the body of Moses. They buried him somewhere in Moabite land east of the Jordan, in a place that remains unknown to this day.

Gone was the man who had taught them the law of justice, the law of worship, the law of ethics, saying, "Remember to love the stranger, for you were strangers in the land of Egypt."

Joshua and all of Israel mourned for thirty days.

·7·
JOSHUA PREPARES THE PEOPLE

In the morning, after a rain, as Joshua stood in the door of his tent praying, the voice of God came to him and said, "Arise now, and prepare to take this nation across the river Jordan in three days, for you shall cause them to inherit the land that I swore to give them. And have no fear, for as I was with Moses, so shall I be with you. I will not forsake you. Be strong and brave, observe the Law that Moses has taught you, and all will go well with you."

Filled with strength and a quiet joy he had never known before, Joshua stood listening as God commanded him to take the land, saying its borders were from the mountains of Lebanon in the north to the desert in the south, and from the great sea in the west to the land east of the Jordan. God named the cities of Canaan and said that Jericho, in the central lands, was the gateway to all the land. He commanded Joshua to take Jericho first, then the city of Ai.

When the spirit of God departed, Joshua knew all that he must do.

"Prepare to leave this tent and move into Moses' tent," he said to Pnina. "The people are accustomed to going there with questions and complaints. They know it as the leader's tent. It will help them grow accustomed to me."

Pnina said she wasn't feeling well. She instructed Carmi and Channa in what to do, and they loaded rugs, blankets, storage jars, cooking vessels, and other household possessions onto donkeys. Joshua did not trust his weapons with just anyone and sent them ahead with Amram. Instead of walking, Pnina mounted the donkey Jochebed was sitting on and rode to Moses' tent. Joshua walked beside them.

Soon Joshua and his family stood in Moses' tent, looking around at their own possessions. Joshua was pleased with his decision. Something of Moses remained. He could almost feel the beloved presence.

"What should be done with the master's possessions?" Carmi asked.

"This, keep here," Joshua said, indicating the case with Joseph's bones. "I have no patience for writing. Take the tablets to the chief scribe. Hereafter, he will keep the record that Moses began."

Joshua purified himself and went to speak with Eleazar.

"God has spoken to me," he told the high priest, "and commanded me to bring the people across the river Jordan in three days. We will arrive in Canaan on the first day of Nisan. Assemble the people, and I will speak to them."

Eleazar instructed the trumpet blowers to sound the call of general assembly. As he and Joshua ascended the hill of the altar, two blasts sounded throughout the camp, and the Israelites came out of their tents.

Joshua was confident of what he had to do but nervous about how the people would react. If even one person expressed fear or doubt, it could spread to others. He would have to go carefully.

"Israelites!" he said, when they were all assembled. "I have this day spoken to God." He had never uttered those words before, and he paused a moment to let them take hold. "Prepare food and drink for yourselves, for in three days we go in to Canaan to possess it."

Behind him, the smoke of the altar rose, and in the stillness he could hear the hiss of the flames.

"We go to fight for the land that God promised Abraham and Sarah to give us, their descendants," he continued. "We will drive out wickedness and make of Canaan a land where God alone is worshiped."

"God do we revere and God will we serve," the people answered.

Joshua was pleased. No one had opposed the journey. He tried to speak forcefully, the way Moses used to do.

"We have nothing to fear, for on our side is the power of God," he said. "God freed your parents from slavery in Egypt and parted the sea for them, so that they might cross over to safety, and drowned the Egyptians who pursued them. God turned away from us the swords and spears that King Og and King Sihon raised against us, and we slew them. When our parents hungered in the desert, God gave them manna and quail to eat. And when they thirsted, God made bitter water sweet for them, and led them to an oasis with seventy palms, where they found twelve springs.

He paused and looked about. Eleazar beamed with approval. And when the people answered with one voice, "God is God in heaven above and on earth below, and there is no other god," Joshua knew he could count on them to be ready to leave in three days.

·8·

CROSSING OVER

On the first day of Nisan, the tents were down and piled on carts, the donkeys were loaded, and the Israelites were ready to march.

Pnina sat beating olives between two stones to get oil. Nearby, Joshua ate barley and vegetables with flat bread, glancing from the corner of his eye at Jochebed and her little cousin, eating beside him. They ate with eyes down, because when they had grown noisy at the thought of leaving and wanted to mount the donkey, he had ordered them to sit still and finish eating in silence.

Pnina handed him a wafer spread with oil, then gave the oil supply to Channa to take along. Amram and Carmi stood folding the tent they had taken down.

"Finished!" Jochebed cried, jumping up. She and her cousin ran to the waiting donkey. Joshua watched as Amram lifted them up, then went to help his mother mount.

The Israelite leader drank the last drops of goat's milk from the cup and rose to look around. All was ready. The people stood beside their donkeys. The Tabernacle poles had been loaded on carts. The altar was covered with a purple cloth for the journey, and the ark with a blue cloth. The ark priests, two in front and two in back, stood ready to lift the staves of the ark and carry it away. Eleazar, running between one group and another, had seen to everything.

Joshua glanced up at the sky. A rain had fallen earlier and the sky was still leaden. He was glad. The absence of sun would make marching easier. He nodded to Caleb, who was standing with his wife, Ephrath, his son Hur, and the rest of his clan amid their carts and donkeys, and went up the hill where the altar had stood.

"Israelites!" he called. "Let us march to the river Jordan and cross over into the Promised Land." He could sense the mood of the people as he ran down the hill. They were excited, eager, fearful of the unknown. He went up to Pnina, the children, and the servants, took his staff, and began the march westward, out of Shittim.

Moses had assigned a marching order to the tribes. Now priests, elders, nobles, and all their households, lined up and followed Joshua out. The morning passed without incident. There were no complaints, no arguments, and, most important, no questions to set off a wave of doubt or regret. Joshua communicated his pleasure to Eleazar and Caleb as they walked along.

But his high spirits did not last. As the people came near the river, they drew back. Jericho rose up in plain view, and the sight unnerved them. They were accustomed to tents in the desert and mud huts in the villages that they passed. But now, on the other side of the river, they saw a great and powerful city with giant buildings. They stood staring, open-mouthed and afraid. A few began to murmur.

Joshua could not let the situation continue. He could not command them to cross over; they were too frightened. He could not risk their refusal. If they disobeyed him, he would be a failed leader, and they would never obey him again.

"Israelites, refresh yourselves," he called, to gain time.

It seemed the right thing to say. They began to call one to the other. Then Joshua told his family to go into the water. They and Caleb with all his clan went, and the people followed, drinking from cupped hands and splashing water on their faces.

Joshua sat down on the banks of the river to think. What would Moses have done to give the people confidence and get them to cross over? As he sat engaged in thought, he heard the voice of God say, "I have promised your ancestors, Abraham and Sarah, to make of them a great nation, and on this day will I commence to make you great."

He remained listening as God spoke on, filling him with wisdom and giving him a plan. Then he rose up on the bank.

"Israelites!" he called. "God has spoken and commanded you to cross over. Behold the sign telling you that you have nothing to fear."

Joshua turned to the priests. "Ark priests, carry the ark into the river."

The ark priests lifted the ark and walked with it to the river, and as they stepped in, lo, the waters drew to one side and left them standing on dry ground.

The people looked and marveled. "It is the sign," they murmured.

"Elders," Joshua called, "choose a strong man from your tribe and let him pick up a stone from the river and carry it to the other side, and let the twelve men build there an altar to God."

The twelve were chosen and went in. Then Pnina and the children and Caleb and his clan went in, and while Joshua watched, they and the multitude crossed over on the dry land where the waters had parted.

The women and children of the tribes of Reuben, Gad, and half of Manasseh remained east of the Jordan, but their men crossed over with the rest, as Moses had arranged. Then Joshua went in and crossed over. And when he and the others stood on the western bank and looked back, they saw the waters begin to return.

·9·

CANAAN, THE PROMISED LAND

The Israelites stood gazing about themselves in silent wonder. They were in Canaan. After more than four hundred years of exile in Egypt, and forty more of wandering in the desert wilderness, they stood on the green, fertile fields of the Promised Land, amid trees laden with fruit.

"Behold, the land that the Lord, your God, has given you," Joshua said. He turned to Pnina, the family, and those standing near. "Here is the wheat and barley of which Moses spoke, the figs, pomegranates, olives, and dates."

The people wept with joy and embraced one another. As Joshua witnessed it and was happy, he remembered the words of Moses: *And when you have arrived in the land of your inheritance, take of the first of all the fruit of the land that God has given you and offer it up as a sacrifice to the Lord.*

Joshua wished his Master and Teacher could have been there with him. He brushed a tear from his eye as he thought about it. Then he embraced Pnina, his children, and the servants, and turned to the people.

"We have this day arrived in the land that God has given us," he said.

"Blessed is the Lord, our God," the people called.

"The wandering is over," Joshua said. "Pitch your tents, O Israelites. Gather up the fruits of the land, a few of each kind, and let us give a thanks offering to the Lord on the altar of twelve stones. We have come to stay."

The priests and the people took up their tasks, and on the plains of Jericho, between the river Jordan and the city of Jericho, the black tents of the Israelites went up in Canaan. As usual, the Tabernacle was set up in the center of the camp.

As Pnina and the family saw to the tent, Joshua stood gazing at the city that God had commanded him to take first. It rose up out of the plains like some great beast and was an hour's march away.

Caleb came up to him. He nodded toward the city. "What will they think, seeing our tents?" he asked.

Joshua paused. "They will send spies to see whose tents they are," he said. He looked away from the city and faced Caleb. "The news of our victory over King Sihon and King Og has traveled over the desert to the plains. The king of Jericho knows it, too. He will not like us so near. He will be wary, but not afraid. For his people outnumber us. And behind those fortified walls, they have nothing to fear."

Joshua glanced about. The new altar of twelve stones was already up. The Israelites were busy with their tents, their children, and their livestock, setting things in order. He smiled at Caleb. "In time, we shall deal with Jericho. For now, we are in the Promised Land. Let us become settled." He looked for Eleazar and saw him. "Eleazar!" he called to the high priest, who came hurrying over.

"Come, Eleazar. Let us give thanks," Joshua said.

The high priest glanced down at his rough garments. "I will put on my priestly robes," he said.

Joshua looked about at the happiness of the people. "The joy of the Israelites is robe enough this day," he said. "Amram!" he called to his son. "Bring some red dye to me at the new altar."

The people followed Joshua and Eleazar to the altar of twelve stones, the first altar to be built in their land. When Amram returned, Joshua dipped a stick into the dye and wrote on the stones the words that the Israelites heard God speak when they came out of Egypt.

I am your God Who brought you out of Egypt
    where you were slaves, and you shall have
    no other god before me.
You shall not worship graven images,
    for I alone am your God.
You shall not speak My name in vain.

Joshua then wrote a copy of the law that Moses received on Mount Sinai.

You shall keep the Sabbath holy, for on it
    God rested from the work of creation.
You shall honor your mother and father.
You shall not murder.
You shall not commit adultery.
You shall not steal.
You shall not swear falsely.
You shall not covet your neighbor's possessions.

When he finished writing, Joshua turned to the people.

"Obey the Law, and all shall go well with you in the land," he said.

"We know the Law and shall obey it," the people answered.

"Remember also the other commandments that God gave you," Joshua said. And he repeated the commandments Moses had told him to teach to the people.

"You shall each give half a sheqel's weight of silver to God. It shall be for the priests, the stranger, the fatherless, and the widow, that all may eat among you and be satisfied.

"Cursed be those who make or worship graven images, who remove a neighbor's landmark, who make the blind to go astray, who take advantage of the stranger, the fatherless, and the widow, and who sin."

"Amen," the people answered.

Eleazar's assistants, the priests, had made a fire in the new altar, and the people who had gone to gather the fruits brought a basket with branches, vines, and plants and set it down before Eleazar.

The high priest took in each hand some branches and vines and said: "A wanderer was our ancestor Jacob when he went to Egypt and fathered a great nation there. The Egyptians made us slaves and afflicted us. We cried out to God, and God heard us and brought us out of Egypt with a mighty hand and sent Moses to deliver us. And Moses led us here to this land that is overflowing with milk and honey."

Eleazar shook the branches and vines and, looking heavenward, said: "God in heaven above and on earth below, Creator of all that is, we give thanks for bringing us to this land and for putting seed into the earth that we might eat."

He threw the vines he held into the flames, then the basket with all its contents, and said, "The mountains, which You made, also thank You for their lives, and also the seas, and the trees sing Your praises."

"Holy, holy, holy are the works of the Lord," the people sang out.

Joshua stepped forward. "And now let us rejoice!" he cried. "Dancers! Where are you?"

"Here, master," Malka, the chief dancer, called. "We hasten to make ready."

The people fell upon each other in rapture, laughing and weeping at the same time, and then sat to form a circle on the ground. The children, too excited to play, leaped and ran without reason.

Joshua saw that Amram was fidgety, turning and looking this way and that.

"Have you lost something?" he asked his son.

"I haven't yet seen . . ." Amram began.

Joshua gave his son an affectionate shove. "Go then and find her," he said.

Amram ran off toward the tents of Benjamin, while Joshua, Pnina, and Jochebed seated themselves in the circle with the others. Channa and Carmi hurried back to the tent to bring food.

Joshua looked at his daughter. Jochebed was weary, yet flushed with excitement.

The sun began its descent, filling the sky with blazing colors. Joshua could sense the excitement around him. But a sweet stillness had settled over him, and he heard none of the murmuring and commotion.

"The dancers!" the people cried.

Their shouts roused Joshua. Channa and Carmi had returned with oiled flat breads and some wine to gladden the heart in celebration. Joshua and Pnina made room for them.

Jochebed could not take her eyes from the dancers. Malka and the others, now in white robes, had reddened their lips and painted their eyes black. They stood in the center of the circle, tambourines held high over their heads. Jochebed turned to Pnina.

"Mother, have you seen what Malka did to her face?"

Pnina sipped from the wine vessel that Joshua held to her lips. "That is how she looks when she dances for the people," she said.

Malka gave a loud wail, breaking it into notes with the rapid movement of her tongue. Then she slapped her tambourine and leaped into the air, setting the bells on her ankles ringing. The other dancers followed.

·10·
CIRCUMCISION IS RENEWED AT GILGAL

Now, one of the commandments that God had given Moses to pass on to Joshua dealt with circumcision. More than five hundred years before, Abraham and Sarah had promised God that all males would be circumcised, as a sign that Israel is pledged to God.

Abraham circumcised himself when he was ninety-nine years old. The vow was kept in the next generation by their son Isaac and Rebeccah, his wife, and in the generation after that. And the promise was kept all the years that the Israelites were in Egypt. But it was not kept in the desert, during the wandering, and God commanded Joshua to renew the vow as soon as the Israelites were settled in Canaan.

The next day, after the morning sacrifice, Joshua spoke from the hill of the altar and told the people of God's command.

"All that God tells us to do will we do," they answered.

They made knives out of flintstones. All the males in the camp, young and old alike, were circumcised.

Joshua often prayed at the door of his tent. And one day as he stood in the doorway speaking what was in his heart, the voice of God came to him and said, "This nation angered Me with its complaints in the desert, but here will I roll away My anger against them."

Joshua named the place Gilgal, which means "rolling away." And there, in their first encampment in Canaan, between Jericho and the river Jordan, the twelve tribes began to live as a settled nation.

In their wandering, they had lived as other nomads did, camping for a while, then breaking camp and moving on. To provide for themselves and to have goods for sale, they wove cloth, made tents and sandals out of animal skins, molded clay vessels to cook and eat with. They forged tools and weapons. Now they had come to remain in one place. And they began also to turn the soil and plant seeds and to tend the trees and vines.

The people toiled for six days, but on the seventh day they rested. And as the fourteenth of Nisan drew near, Joshua reminded them of the coming of Passover, and they began the special preparations for it. They slaughtered lambs and roasted them. And they cooked the same foods that their parents had eaten during the wandering.

At dusk, on the fourteenth of Nisan, the Israelites came out of their tents, spread their cloths under the stars, and brought out the food that they had prepared.

Joshua sat with his clan before his tent. All were there— the married sons and daughters with their children, Pnina, Jochebed, Amram, Carmi, and Channa. In front of them, on a clay plate, were morsels of roasted lamb. On other plates were the unleavened cakes and parched corn that their parents had eaten in the desert. For the adults there was strong wine to drink, and for the children the juice of pomegranates.

As the family ate, spooning up the parched corn with pieces of unleavened bread or reaching for a morsel of lamb, Joshua spoke to them of the time that the Israelites were slaves in Egypt and of how Moses had led them out. The children listened attentively, sometimes forgetting to eat.

Thus did all the Israelites celebrate their first Passover in the Promised Land.

·11·
RAHAB

After the Passover, when the rains of winter were gone, Joshua turned his thoughts to Jericho. He had seen the city some ten years before when he and Caleb and the others went to spy out the land for Moses. He knew that it would be about an hour's march from Gilgal, and that a mud brick wall enclosed the city and protected it. But he would have to know something about the inhabitants of the city before he could plan for attack.

When the evening meal was over, he sent for two spies.

"Go into Jericho and walk about the marketplace," he told them. "Listen to what people say and learn what you can about their mood, the king, and the size of his army."

The spies left at dawn. They arrived about an hour later at

the large wooden gates of Jericho. Visitors were going in and out. The spies joined those who were entering. Inside the gate, the shops and stalls were busy. The spies bought water to drink from a vender, then walked about, looking, listening, asking questions.

From the potter they learned that the king had a large army. From a public scribe seated in front of a building they learned that the king kept a close watch on the city because he knew that Joshua, the slayer of King Og and King Sihon, was now encamped on this side of the river.

At the dye house the spies asked where they could find an inn. They were told that a woman named Rahab kept an inn at the entrance to the city, near the gates.

The spies went to the inn and ordered food. Rahab was at first unfriendly. But when she brought them soup and asked them who they were, and they told her they were Israelites, her mood changed. She called to her helper to take care of the other customers, and sat down to speak with the spies.

"I know of your people," she said proudly. "Four hundred years ago there was a famine here in Canaan. Your ancestor, Jacob, lived then south of here in Hebron. And when there was no food to eat, he left and went with his clan of seventy to Egypt, where food was plentiful and where Joseph, his son, was adviser to the king."

The spies looked at each other in surprise. How could this woman of Jericho know that?

"My parents taught it to me. Their parents taught it to them," she said, as if in answer to their unspoken question.

"Moses, our leader and teacher, kept a history of our people," one of the spies said. "It is written that the seventy who left were all the population."

The second spy looked at Rahab. "Since it was spoken of in your home, can it be that not everyone left with Jacob? That some stayed behind and adopted the ways of the Canaanites?"

Rahab smiled. "I do not know," she said. "The people here worship many gods. I worship none." She thought a moment. "Jacob left, but he returned," she added. "He is buried in Hebron, with his wife and parents. His sons, too."

Suddenly her young brother came running in from the street.

"The water carrier recognized these two as Israelite spies, and the king's men are on the way here to seize them," he said to Rahab.

Rahab turned to the spies. "Come with me to the roof," she said. "That is where I dry flax to make cotton. No one will look there."

She led the spies to the roof and hid them under the stalks of flax, concealing them well. Then she went down to await the soldiers.

They were soon at the door. "Two Israelites were seen entering here," they said.

Rahab shrugged. "This is a public house. People come and go here," she said. "Two strangers came; I do not know who they are. They had a meal, paid, and left. That is all I know." She nodded toward the city gates. "I saw them head that way. If you hurry, you might catch them."

The soldiers left, and Rahab sent her brother to follow

after them. He returned in the evening to say the soldiers had looked and given up the search.

Rahab called to the spies to come down from the roof and tied a scarlet cord to the back window.

"You can leave now," she said and went to the window. She tugged at the cord. "Lower yourselves. You will not be seen in back. Only hurry. The sun is going down, and the gatekeeper will be closing the gates at any moment."

The spies thanked her and hurried to the window.

"The people here know that your god is God in heaven above and on earth below, and they fear you," Rahab said.

"We will remember your kindness," the spies said. "Let the scarlet cord remain hanging as a sign that this is your house."

They climbed out the window, first one, then the other, lowered themselves to the ground, and hastened out of the city through the still-open gates.

·12·
THE WALL

Joshua's tent was dark and silent with sleeping forms. But he could find no rest. He was elated with the news the spies had brought back. He had heard them out with interest and sent them to bed. From what they had to say, circumstances in Jericho were in his favor. Since the king feared him, and the people feared God, his task was made easy, if he could get inside the city. But how was he to do that? A wall surrounded the city. He had no battering rams to knock it down, no tools to dig under it and so topple it. He was confident of his skills as a warrior. Enemy after enemy had fallen before his sword. But nothing in his experience had prepared him for this.

Silently, so as not to wake the others, he rose from his mat and went to seek the counsel of God. He washed his hands and feet in the brass laver outside the Tabernacle and went in.

Even as he entered, a peace descended on him. Parting the curtains to the second chamber, he went into the holy of holies and fell on his face before the ark to speak what was in his heart.

When he rose, he knew what to do. The presence of God had appeared to him and given him a plan.

Joshua returned to his tent and slept for what remained of the night. He awoke refreshed. "Rise!" he called to the children in the morning. He cleansed himself with oil, put on a cotton robe, and went from the tent.

Outside, Pnina had spread a cloth on the ground for the morning meal. Joshua was hungry and looked eagerly at the bowl of boiled wheat and another of dates. Pnina sat by the fire in deep concentration, baking flat round breads.

"Your fire is in need of tinder," Joshua said, looking at the feeble flame.

Pnina looked up. "I was listening to it sputter and complain of having to do the work of many. Carmi has gone for some tinder." She smiled at him. "Can you be rested?" she asked. "It was almost light when you returned to your mat."

Joshua seated himself on the cloth. He cared deeply for Pnina and often spoke to her of what was in his heart. "I could not find a way to enter Jericho," he said. "My thoughts churned and churned without purpose. I sought the presence of the Lord for guidance." He paused. "We go into Jericho this very day. I will speak to the people of it after the morning sacrifice," he added, and took a date from the bowl.

Carmi returned with a supply of dried goat dung and added some squares to the fire. Channa appeared from another direction with water from the well. Amram and Jochebed came out of the tent, and all sat down to the morning meal.

"Father," Amram said, "I heard you tell Mother that we go into Jericho this day. May I go, too?"

"And who will guard the pretty girls of the tribe of Benjamin?" Joshua teased.

Amram blushed. "I will soon be eleven," he said. "Why should I stay home with the children and listen to Mother teach Jochebed and other small ones how to read in the tablets?"

"Then practice throwing stones and using your slingshot," Joshua answered. "You will need those skills in the wars that lie ahead."

Joshua finished eating and went to the hill of the altar. There, after the morning sacrifice, he told the people of the plan God had given him to take Jericho.

·13·
JERICHO

The day became pleasantly cool. Joshua had assigned a marching order, and there was a great milling about as the Israelites arranged themselves by tribe. At last, the people stood shoulder to shoulder with others of their tribe. The priests took places in back of them. Eleazar, in his priestly robes, lead the priests who carried the ark. Behind them were seven other priests, each with a ram's horn.

Joshua signaled the trumpet blower to give the starting blast, and the blast was heard. "To Jericho!" he called, leading the people across the plains of Jericho and up toward the city.

In the marching order assigned to them, the Israelites walked around the wall of Jericho while the priests blew softly and continuously on their horns. When they had circled the city once, Joshua led them back to Gilgal.

In the evening, he and Caleb and other elders spoke of the march as they sat before Joshua's tent.

"It went as you said it would, Joshua," Caleb said.

"Yes," Eleazar agreed. "The king and his men made no move, just watched us from the rooftops and did nothing."

Joshua nodded. "They had no cause for alarm," he said. "They saw no weapons or signs of war, just Israelites marching with their ark. They see our God as strange, and our customs as stranger still. To them, it was a strange form of worship."

Channa, the maidservant, placed bowls of fruit before the gathering. Joshua helped himself to a fig. "We shall do the same every day for five more days," he said. "We will so accustom them to the sight of us that they will no longer pay any attention to us. Then we shall deliver a surprise."

Each day for the next five days, Joshua led the Israelites in a march around Jericho, and each evening they returned to Gilgal. It happened as Joshua had said. By the fourth day, the king and his men were gone from the rooftops and the people no longer found the sight of interest. By the sixth day, not a single head bothered to turn to look at the Israelites. Joshua had created in Jericho the mood he had striven for. He was now ready to attack.

The next morning, the people gathered as usual for the sacrifice. Joshua stood on the hill beside Eleazar. When the sacrifice was over, Joshua spoke to the people.

"Israelites," he said. "Hide daggers and swords in your robes, for this day we go into Jericho to take it!"

Achan, one of Joshua's officers, spoke from below as a murmur of excitement arose.

"But what of the wall?" he asked. "How are we to get into the city?"

"Only trust in God, and do as I say," Joshua answered.

"God has commanded you how to behave in Jericho," he said. "You are to spare the trees and herds. You may take for yourself, as spoils of war, flocks, furniture, and household goods. But you may not take treasure. This is for the Tabernacle, where the spirit of God comes sometimes to rest. Listen well. You are forbidden to touch any silver or gold or vessels of iron or brass. They belong to God.''

Joshua paused, allowing the words to take hold. ''This, too, I command,'' he said. ''Spare Rahab, who hid the spies, her and all her clan. Her house is near the gate. A scarlet cord hangs from the window.''

''It shall be done, Joshua,'' the people answered with one voice.

''You will march around the city until I tell you to stop,'' Joshua said. ''And you will speak no word and utter no sound until I say, 'Shout!' ''

Joshua went down from the hill, and the Israelites returned to their tents for weapons. When the people were again assembled, Joshua led them out to Jericho. There, as ordered, the Israelites marched around the city in silence. No one spoke or uttered a sound. The only noise that came from them was the soft and continuous blowing of the rams' horns.

When they had circled the wall, Joshua gave the signal. ''Shout!'' he cried. ''God has given you the city!''

The Israelites shouted with a thousand voices, and the priests with horns gave a great and resounding blast until, suddenly, the wall of Jericho came loose from the earth and fell down flat.

The people of Jericho, unexpectedly revealed, stood staring in disbelief.

Joshua had been waiting for this moment. God had shown it to him in the Tabernacle. ''Go in and take the city,'' he cried to the Israelites. ''It is yours!''

Running and shouting with upraised swords, the Israelites swarmed into the city and smote the stunned inhabitants. They knocked down all the idols worshiped there, breaking them to pieces, and also the altars at which the people of Jericho burned their children in sacrifice.

Joshua sent the two spies to see to it that Rahab was safe. "Set fire to the city!" he then called to the men nearest him.

Joshua stood at the edge of the city watching the flames rise, while in the interior of the city, his officer, Achan, found himself alone and unobserved before the house of the slain king. As all about him people ran every which way, shouting and yelling in confusion, Achan hurried into the house. He stole two hundred sheqels of silver and a wedge of gold and hid them among the spoils of war that he was permitted to take.

At the end of the day, Joshua rose up on some fallen stones to survey the ruins. He had reduced the city to a heap and a rubble, as God had commanded him to do. This had been the largest city in the central lands. It no longer stood to block his way. Now Joshua could enter deeper into Canaan.

He glanced around. There was nothing more to be done. Eleazar had gone about with the priests to claim the treasures for the Tabernacle. The people stood surrounded by their spoils.

"Israelites!" he called. "Take your cattle and the flocks that you have inherited in battle, and let us return to our tents."

Joshua led the people out. They sang and shouted as they went, driving their herds before them. Rahab and her clan, with all their possessions, were among them.

·14·
GOD IS ANGERED

Joshua let the people rest after battle, then turned his thoughts to Ai, the city that God had commanded him to take next. He knew little about the place and sent his spies to search it out. Since he did not know how far it was, he did not know when to expect them back. He waited all day. In the evening, he sat before his tent with members of his tribe and others, awaiting their return. Caleb was also with him.

The spies returned late at night. They told Joshua and those who were with him what they had learned. Ai was situated at the top of a canyon, a walk of some five or six hours from Gilgal. It had fewer people than Jericho and was less well fortified. The inhabitants of the city knew what Joshua had done in Jericho and were afraid of him.

Joshua listened with interest. Pleased, he turned to the others. "Our task has been made easy," he said. "Fear will make the people of Ai ripe for defeat. The war will be very short and will require few men." He turned to Caleb. "It is not a matter for the entire army," he said. "You, Caleb, with a select group of mighty men, can take the city. Return to your tent to sleep. At dawn, go up to Ai and take it! And may God be with you."

Caleb said good night and left. At dawn, he prepared for the journey and gathered his men.

But God was not with them. God was angry because Achan had stolen from Jericho treasures that had been set aside for the Tabernacle. And His anger was upon all of Israel for the deed. And when Caleb and his men arrived at Ai and went up the walls of the canyon, God withheld success from them.

The warriors of Ai fell upon them and slew almost all of them. Caleb was among those who were driven back. Bloodied and covered with dirt, he led the few who still lived back to Gilgal.

When Joshua saw them and heard of the defeat, he wept. God had promised not to forsake him, yet he had been forsaken. He ran from his tent to the Tabernacle and fell on his face before the ark.

"Why have You delivered us from Egypt and brought us across the Jordan, only to cause us to perish? Our enemies now know we can be beaten, and they will surely destroy us!" he said.

The voice of God answered. "Why are you fallen on your face? Rise up. The people have stolen and lied in Jericho, and I have therefore put a curse on them. Go before them and say I will not be with them until the guilty one among them has been destroyed."

Joshua trembled with anger. Who had dared disobey him? Who had trampled on God's command? He went from the Tabernacle and told Eleazar to assemble the people. And as he ascended the hill to speak, one trumpet blast followed another.

Standing alone on the hill, Joshua watched the people come out of their tents. Many mighty men had been slain, and a mood of sorrow and grieving was upon them, as it was upon him.

"God has told me why our mighty men have fallen," he said. "When we went into Jericho, I repeated to you God's words, to take what was permitted to you but to touch no silver or gold. These belong to the Tabernacle, I told you. Yet someone has stolen silver and gold, and the wrath of God is upon us."

The people listened in silence.

"These words has God commanded me to say to you," Joshua continued. " 'Tell them I will not be with them until the guilty one among them has been destroyed.' "

A murmuring arose from the crowd as Achan came forward.

"I have sinned against the God of Israel," he said. "I have taken two hundred sheqels of silver and a wedge of gold and hidden them in the earth, in the midst of my tent."

"Amram," Joshua called to his son. "Go with Carmi to Achan's tent and bring back what you find."

Amram and the servant went and soon returned with the silver and gold, which they spread out on the ground before Joshua and all the people.

Shouts of anger arose.

"Seize him and blot out his name from under the sun," Joshua said.

Achan's life was ended in the manner of the time, without burial in the earth and with no one to mourn for him. He and his clan were taken to the valley outside the camp.

They were stoned to death. Then they and their possessions were burned by fire until nothing was left.

Joshua called the place Achor, which means "troubled place," and it is so called to this day.

·15·
"TAKE IT, IT IS YOURS"

Once more winter came, bringing rains to the parched earth. Joshua was grateful for the season. The light rains were a time to plant, the heavy rains a time to cease from making war. He was glad for the rest. It was not weariness of body that had overtaken him, but of spirit. The defeat at Ai had left him morose, frightened even.

No one saw his mood. He seemed his usual self as he went about the camp settling disputes between the tribes, visiting the sick. The sacrifices also kept him busy. Apart from the daily morning and evening sacrifices at the holy altar, which he attended faithfully, special sacrifices took place all day long.

From early morning people came with a loaf of bread, a cake of oiled bread, or a wafer of unleavened bread to offer up to God as thanks for some happy event. Joshua could not attend them all, for they were too many, but he went whenever he could. Doing so served two purposes. He could show a confident face to the people. He could also learn about happenings around the camp.

The same was true of the guilt sacrifices. Eleazar conducted these at a public altar, outside the camp. As people confessed a sin or wrongdoing, Joshua learned about their character and the problems they faced. And, from the offering, he knew how rich a person was. The very rich atoned with a bullock, the less rich with a sheep or dove, the poor with a simple meal offering.

Joshua was careful to keep his feelings to himself, especially when he was with Pnina. She had not been feeling well. It was plain from the lack of vitality with which she wove cloth or mashed corn. Joshua tried to amuse her by speaking of births, betrothals, and other camp gossip.

Only when he was alone did he allow his feelings to rule. Again and again he tormented himself with the same dark thoughts. Moses would never have been so arrogant as to use only part of the army to take Ai. Achan would never have dared disobey Moses. What pained Joshua was his loss of reputation. He had always been successful in battle. But now, because he had been defeated, he was no longer feared.

He prayed in the doorway of his tent, asking God's guidance. Weeks passed, and the rains began to lessen and the sun to reassert itself in the sky. And one morning, as he stood in the doorway of his tent speaking what was in his heart, the voice of God came to him and said, "Go now against Ai, fear not, but go up there and take it, for it is yours."

Joshua listened as God spoke on, filling him with wisdom and telling him what to do. When the voice of God had departed, Joshua hurried to the hill of the altar and spoke to the people.

"Israelites," he said. "I have this day spoken to God, and we go into Ai, this time to possess it. God has given me a plan for success."

He was pleased to see that the people were attentive.

"This is the plan," he continued. "Caleb and some mighty men will go at once and hide behind the city. All others, warriors and children aged eleven and older, will follow me toward Ai. When we arrive and the king sees how numerous we are, he will think all of Israel marches against him. He will send his entire army out to slay us, leaving his city undefended. When I give the signal, the mighty men will go into the city and take it!"

Joshua could sense the excitement of the crowd. His eye fell on Amram, standing between Pnina and Jochebed. Amram was grinning. He was eleven and could not hide his pleasure at the thought of going.

"Caleb," Joshua said, "I will speak with you and the mighty men before you depart." He paused and looked about. "And now, Israelites, to your tents to prepare."

The people returned to their tents, and he descended the hill. A few Israelites waited for him with questions, and he answered them all. Then he went to his tent. When he arrived, he found that Amram had already filled skins with water and pomegranate juice for both of them and that Channa and Pnina had prepared sacks of dry food to take along.

"Can I go too, Father?" Jochebed asked.

"And leave your mother alone?" Joshua said.

Jochebed glanced away. "When *will* I be able to go?" she asked.

"When you are bigger."

Pnina took Jochebed by the hand. "We will have a good time," she said. "We will go to the tent of your cousins. Grandfather will tell you and the other children the stories you like to hear."

Joshua and Amram embraced Pnina, Jochebed, and the servants and left. Outside, the mighty men stood ready with swords and spears. Joshua went up to them.

"Hide yourselves behind the city," he said, "not so close that you will be seen, nor so far that you will not see me, for I will signal you from the city. Remain alert. Do not take your eyes from me. When you see me raise my sword, come in and take the city!"

Caleb and the mighty men left. Amram tried to go with them, but Joshua called him back and told him his place was with the people. When the donkeys were loaded and all stood ready to leave, Joshua led them out of Gilgal, marching west with them in the direction of the sea.

When they arrived at Ai, it was as Joshua had said. The entire army of Ai had been sent out.

"They come, running and shouting and waving their swords," Joshua said. "Do not stay and fight. Turn and flee into the wilderness."

The Israelites turned and fled, and the soldiers followed them into the wilderness. But Joshua remained behind. In the confusion, he slipped unnoticed into the city. And when

he found an empty house from which he could be seen by the mighty men hiding behind the city, he stood in the doorway and raised his sword.

In an instant, the mighty men came swarming into the city and took it. They destroyed the idols and altars and set fire to the city.

When the soldiers of Ai looked back from the wilderness

and saw flames rising from the city, their hearts went out of them. The Israelites turned around and slew them and returned to the city. Amram was among them.

"Israelites!" Joshua cried. "We have taken Ai and made of it a heap and a rubble. The victory is not ours but belongs to God!"

"Blessed is our God, Who gives victory," the people answered.

Joshua built an altar of unhewn stones to God and on it wrote a copy of the Law that had been given to Moses. Then he and the Israelites returned to Gilgal, driving before them the flocks and herds they had taken from Ai.

A feast had been prepared to celebrate the victory. And that night, as women danced and musicians played under the stars, Joshua sat outside his tent with all his household, eating roast lamb with beans and vegetables and sipping wine to further gladden his heart.

·16·

A GOAT IS SACRIFICED

Joshua was now famous in all the land and also greatly feared. The Hivites especially had reason to fear him. He was marching westward toward the sea to conquer the central lands. And the only city still standing in that region was their capital, Gibeon.

Fearing for their lives, the Hivites of four cities met in Gibeon and arrived at a plan. They would trick Joshua into giving them a peace treaty. Since he would not make peace with a Canaanite nation that he had vowed to destroy, they would pretend to be from elsewhere. They prepared to carry out this plan.

Three elders put on dusty robes and torn sandals and smeared their donkeys with mud. The wineskins they took were old, resewn, and patched together. Disguised as weary travelers, they set out on their journey. Gilgal was less than half a day's march away. But when they arrived at the Israelite camp, they seemed, from the dust and mud, to have been traveling for days.

As travelers, they were made welcome at the camp. Carmi, hearing they wished to see Joshua, poured water over their hands and gave them pomegranate juice to drink, then brought them into Joshua's tent.

Joshua came from behind the curtain, where he had been sitting with Pnina and the children.

"These travelers wish to speak with you, master," Carmi said.

The men bowed.

"From what land are you?" Joshua asked, observing the dusty robes.

"We have journeyed for many days to reach you," one answered. "Our land is far away, over the border. But our people have heard that your God is powerful, and they have sent us to ask you for a peace treaty."

Joshua was pleased and would have accepted. But he waited to speak with the elders. To avoid their criticism, he had appointed a council of elders to help him decide important matters. "If it is their decision, too, they will be less likely to complain if it goes badly," he had said to Caleb at the time.

"I will speak with our elders," he said. "Feel at home. Refresh yourselves. Carmi, my servant, will bring you food and drink."

He went from the tent. The peace treaty won easy acceptance. The elders themselves spoke of the benefits to be had from friendly neighbors. All agreed.

"Very well," Joshua said. "We shall bind it with an oath of treaty in the Tabernacle courtyard. I will bring the travelers. Meet us there."

He returned to his tent and found the visitors partaking of figs and lentil patties. "Good appetite," he said. "I have fine news. The elders have agreed to a treaty. We shall sacrifice a she-goat to bind it."

"Blessings upon your God and your people," the spokesman for the three answered.

Joshua turned to Carmi. "Go to Eleazar and tell him to prepare a she-goat for sacrifice."

Hearing those words, Amram came running from behind the curtain, with Jochebed behind him.

"Father, are they going to prepare a she-goat now?" Jochebed asked.

"At this very moment," Joshua answered.

"How good!" Jochebed cried. Amram ran out of the tent toward the courtyard, and his sister followed.

Joshua went behind the curtain to speak to Pnina, then led the men out to the courtyard. An altar of stones had been set up for the treaty sacrifice. A slaughtered goat had been cleaned and its parts placed within its carcass, which lay across the stones. Jochebed and Amram and the other children enjoyed the sight and were in high spirits. People came from all directions to watch the ceremony.

Eleazar lit a fire under the goat and spoke the words of the sacrifice. Then Joshua placed his hands over the hands of the men and said, "You will be as family to us. You will worship our God and obey the laws of our God. In exchange, we shall treat you as our own and allow no harm to come to you."

The three men bowed to Joshua and Eleazar and to all those present. They had succeeded in obtaining a treaty with the Israelites. Now they had nothing to fear.

"We rejoice in your friendship and promise ours in return," the spokesman said.

All sat together and ate and drank. Joshua then gave the travelers food and drink for the journey and sent them on their way.

·17·
THE HIVITES

Some days later, Joshua assembled the army and went out with them toward the sea to make war against Gibeon. As usual, his people entered the city with shouts and upraised swords, but the inhabitants did not fight back. In-

stead they linked arms and looked on in silence.

Such a thing had never happened before. Joshua glanced about, uncomprehending. His surprise turned to anger when he saw the three men with whom he had sworn an oath of treaty.

"Who are you?" he demanded.

"We are Hivites," one answered.

"Why did you pretend to be from a distant land?"

"To save our lives. We know your God has commanded you to destroy the inhabitants of this land."

The Israelites began to shout in anger. "They have lied to us! Let us slay them!" they said.

Joshua raised a hand to silence his men. "We have sworn an oath of treaty and may not harm them," he said. He turned to the Hivites. "You have lied to us and deceived us," he said.

"We are in your hands," the Hivites answered. "Do as it seems right in your sight to do to us."

"As punishment, your nations shall be servants and you shall chop wood and carry water all the days of your lives," Joshua declared.

Joshua and the Israelites returned to Gilgal. Without having to raise a sword, Joshua had inherited Gibeon and the three lesser Hivite cities of Chephirah, Beeroth, and Kiriath-Jearim, and was now in full control of the central lands.

·18·

GIBEON

The moon was full and the night starry as Joshua and his clan sat outside his tent eating figs and dates and sipping pomegranate juice. Amram's friend, the Benjaminite girl, was with them. Jochebed and the children played with stones nearby.

Suddenly the sound of running feet made everyone look up.

A Hivite courier, surrounded by Israelite guards, came running. The courier bowed before Joshua.

"Help us, master," he said. "Five Amorite kings with all their armies are marching against us."

"Why?" Joshua asked.

"Before you arrived, we were allies of the Amorites," the courier answered. "When the Amorite king of Jerusalem heard that we had made a treaty with you, he rose up in anger against us and called upon all the Amorite kings to go out with him in battle against us."

Joshua looked away. Who were the Hivites that he should disturb himself for them? They had lied to him and acted basely. Yet he had killed a she-goat with them and must go to their defense.

"Assemble the army," he called to the guards, and went inside with his family to prepare.

Pnina and Channa filled sacks with food and drink while Jochebed ran between them, trying to help. Joshua went behind the curtain to put on his battle tunic. As he tied the sash around his waist, he began to worry. This was a war between Hivites and Amorites. God had not commanded him to fight it. He slipped his sword under his sash and came out.

Pnina handed Amram a robe. "You will need it for the nights," she said. Amran took the robe and the supplies, then kissed his mother and went out. Jochebed ran out after him to watch.

Joshua embraced Pnina, then, as was his custom, stopped in the doorway of the tent to pray. And as he stood speaking what was in his heart, the voice of God came to him and said, "Fear not, for I have delivered the Amorites into your hands." Joshua listened as God told him what to do. Then he went out into the night.

The full moon lit up the tents and the Israelites who stood before them, watching, and also those who were gathering for battle. Amram was standing with the people of Ephraim. Joshua climbed up the hill of the altar.

"Israelites!" he called. "We go out against five Amorite nations who pray to idols and burn their children in idol worship. We go to slay them and destroy their idols and altars and to build new altars to God."

"As you command, so shall we do," the people answered.

Joshua went down from the hill and led the Israelites out of Gilgal and into the wilderness where jackals brayed and wild things darted before them.

As the sky began to grow light, they arrived at the Amorite camp. Joshua spoke to the people. "Have no fear, but go in and fight!" he said.

And they went in and fell upon the five Amorite armies and fought with them all day. Hailstones fell from the sky on the Amorite camp, killing many. At the end of the day, half the Amorites lay dead and the other half were fleeing into the wilderness.

Joshua, surrounded by his officers and men, watched

them. "We must not allow them to get away," he said. "They will reassemble and attack again."

"Then we must go after them," Caleb said.

"No," Joshua answered. "It is growing dark. They will hide in caves for the night. By the time we arrive, it will be too dark to see."

Amram came running. "Father, the five kings have hidden themselves in a cave," he said.

"Tell the soldiers to guard them," Joshua said. "I will deal with them later."

Amram ran off.

Joshua was aware that the people were waiting for him to make a decision. He looked about at the gathering darkness and whispered, "If only we had more daylight."

He went off by himself and pleaded with God. He spoke softly, from his heart. "Look forth from Your holy habitation, and bless Your people, Israel, and the land You have given us. Lord, extend for us the light of day." He gazed heavenward. Then, speaking aloud, so that everyone might take heart, he said, "Sun, stand still over Gibeon; moon, remain in your place."

Lo, it happened as he had requested. The sun stood still while a whole day passed. And in a light of day never seen before or since, Joshua and the Israelites went out into the wilderness and found the Amorites, every one of them, and slew them all.

As Joshua and the Israelites returned, the sun finished its descent and night came to the sky. Joshua arrived at his tent and fell into a deep sleep.

In the morning, he had each king hanged from a separate tree and left them hanging all day, to show how God dealt with the enemies of Israel.

In the evening, the bodies of the kings were taken down and cast back into the cave. Great stones were rolled in front of the cave to seal it, and their bones are there to this day.

·19·

FESTIVAL
OF THE NEW MOON

The years passed as Joshua and the Israelites made war in the dry months, planted before and after the rains, and gathered in the crops in their season.

Amram married the Benjaminite girl and became a father himself. Jochebed was betrothed to the son of one of the high priests. Joshua worried about Pnina while he was away making war and spent as much time as he could with her during the rainy season, sitting with her in the comfort of the tent and telling stories to the children of the clan as she listened.

In the early spring, before going out to make war, Joshua returned to the tent from a birth celebration. Pnina was reclining against some pillows, eating lentil soup that Channa had prepared for her.

"Another Israelite has been added to the tribe of Ephraim," he said.

"What did they name the child?" Pnina asked.

"Deborah," Joshua answered. "The wise women say she was born with signs and that she will rise to be a judge in Israel."

Pnina smiled. "They are often right," she said. "I thought I would attend the Festival of the New Moon this evening," she added, "but I am too tired."

"I'm sorry," Joshua said. "It is my favorite holiday."

"Yours and the children's," Pnina said.

"It gives me pleasure to hear them laugh."

"You are right," Pnina said. "The Festival of Weeks, Passover, the Sabbath, these have meaning for us, the parents. The children enjoy the light-heartedness of the Festival of the New Moon most."

Joshua cleansed himself and went to join Eleazar on the hill of the altar. After a lamb had been offered up for the evening sacrifice, he went before the crowd and glanced at the faces of the children and their parents in the courtyard below.

He spoke to the people. "These were God's words," he said. " 'And it shall come to pass that from one new moon to another, and from one Sabbath to another, all people shall worship before Me.' "

He looked at the children. "We have worshiped as God has commanded us. Now let us celebrate."

The children sent up shouts of delight.

"Who can tell us why we celebrate?" Joshua asked.

"I can," a little girl answered.

"Then tell us."

"Long ago, when our grandparents came out of Egypt and wandered in the desert, they made a golden calf while Moses was away and worshiped it."

"That's right," Joshua said. "Anything else?"

"I know," a little boy called. Joshua nodded.

"The men gave their golden ornaments to make the

golden calf, but the women did not. They refused," the boy said.

"Can I tell?" a little girl asked. Joshua said she could.

"When Moses came back and saw the golden calf, he was angry and he cursed the men and told them to honor the women at the Festival of the New Moon."

"You have all learned the story well," Joshua said. "The women were given freedom from work on this day. Now the men must prepare the food and do the women's work. Come, let us honor the women," he added, and went down from the hill.

The camp rang with laughter as children watched their fathers struggle to draw water from the well, weave cloth, grind meal, and do the work of women. Joshua told the children who followed him about that he would bake some bread. And he placed the portable stove over the cooking pit and lit the fire. The children could not stop laughing when he cried out each time he burned his fingers trying to remove a newly baked flat bread from the stove.

·20·
JABIN

Joshua was gone from the central lands for many years, fighting in the south for the cities that God had commanded him to take. When the fighting was over, he had conquered Makkedah, Libnah, Lachish, Gezer, Eglon, Hebron, and Debir.

In each city he built an altar to God and wrote on it a copy of the Law, and in each place he left behind a community of people to build a new city that was dedicated to God.

The Israelites made houses from stones that had fallen in battle. Where there were no stones, they built two-story mud brick houses with flat roofs, such as they had seen in Jericho, with large jars under the roof to catch the rain, to provide themselves with a supply of water for the dry season.

Over the years, Joshua made war during the dry season and returned to Gilgal to rest during the rains. In that time, Jochebed married and Pnina died. Some time later, Joshua took Rahab, who had hidden the spies in Jericho, for a wife.

When he had won all the southern lands, Joshua returned to Gilgal to remain for a while. Or so he hoped. But not long after his return, some of his soldiers came running one night to wake him from a deep sleep.

"Canaanites with chariots are marching against us," they said. "They are encamped by the waters of Merom."

Joshua was angry at being awakened. "Who is their leader?" he asked.

One of his officers spoke. "While you were away fighting in the south, a mighty Canaanite king arose in the north, in the city of Hazor. Jabin is his name. They say he has nine hundred chariots," the man said.

"Our spies told us that he thought you were gone from the central lands forever," another officer added. "And when he learned you were back, he called upon the other

Canaanite kings to go out with him in battle."

"I long to rest, but it is not to be," Joshua said. He rose from his mat and ordered the army assembled. And as he dressed for battle, he thought about the nine hundred chariots. Each held two soldiers, one to drive the horse and the other to shoot arrows. A charioteer was able to fight and run at the same time. His men had only swords and shields.

What chance did they have against such a foe?

On the way out, he prayed in the doorway of the tent and spoke his fears, and the voice of God came to him and said, "Be not afraid, go out to them and destroy their horses and burn their chariots, for I will deliver them up slain before Israel."

Joshua went out into the dark to his waiting army and marched with them through the night until they arrived at the Canaanite camp by the waters of Merom. The camp was still, and the men guarding the horses dozed.

Joshua whispered to his men, "Steal up on the guards and slay them, and slay the horses before they become wild with fear and begin to cry out," he said.

The men stole up on the guards and slew them and slew the horses as well.

"Now they, too, will have only swords and shields to fight with," Joshua said. "Follow me, but go softly and in silence," he added, leading them into the camp.

"Attack while they are still asleep and cannot put on their armor," he said. "Now go in!"

The Israelites went in and fell upon the sleeping Canaanites in their tents and fought with them for a long time. During the fighting, Jabin fled to his city for safety. When the fighting was over, Joshua followed Jabin to Hazor and set fire to the city. The king and all the inhabitants of the city were destroyed and their idols and altars with them.

Joshua remained in the north fighting with king after king. After the wars were over, he had inherited the cities of the north that he had been commanded to take, as well as the hills and wilderness around them.

And when Joshua returned to Gilgal, he was in full control of the central, southern, and northern lands of Canaan.

·21·

LOTS ARE CAST AT SHILOH

Joshua made war for twenty-five years and inherited thirty-one of the cities that God had commanded him to take, and in those cities and the lands around them, idols were gone and God was worshiped. Though too old for battle, Joshua was yet in command.

One spring day as he sat outside his tent watching the shepherds return with their flocks, the voice of God came to him and said, "You are old and stricken in years, and there yet remains much land to be taken. Go now to Shiloh and cast lots to divide up the land that has so far been won."

Joshua listened to God's other commands, and when God had finished speaking, Joshua assembled the people and told them to go to Shiloh, where lots would be cast and where the Tabernacle and the ark would henceforth dwell.

Under a cloudless sky, Joshua led the way out of Gilgal. Behind him were Eleazar, the Tabernacle priests with the Tabernacle, the ark priests with the ark, and the altar priests with the altar and all its utensils. The elders and their people followed.

At Shiloh, when they had pitched their tents, Joshua rose

up to speak to the people. "The scribes will take up thirty-one stones, one for each city that we have taken, and write on each stone the name of a city, and they will bring the stones to Eleazar for casting," he said.

The scribes wrote on the stones and brought them to Eleazar, and he cast them out and called the tribes by name.

To the tribes of Simeon, Judah, Issachar, Ephraim, Benjamin, Zebulon, Dan, Asher, Naphtali, and Joseph-Manasseh went the lands in the south, north, and central part of Canaan.

Joshua fulfilled Moses' command and gave the grassy lands east of the river Jordan to the tribes of Reuben, Gad, and the other half of Manasseh, whose men had fought to the end. And to Caleb he gave Hebron, saying, "It shall be a link between our ancient parents and generations yet unborn. Abraham bought from Ephron of that city the Cave of Machpelah as a burial ground, and he and Sarah are buried there. With them lie Isaac, their son, and Rebeccah, his wife, and their son Jacob, and also his wife, Leah."

Joshua then fulfilled God's other commands. "The priests shall have no land of their own but shall receive from each tribe land on which to dwell, with open space around it for their cattle," he said.

And he called for lots to be cast for six cities of refuge, and lots were cast and six such cities were named, three on the east side of the Jordan and three on the west. These were places of safety. Someone who had accidentally killed another could flee there and be safe from the wrath of the stricken family, until a judge could come to judge fairly.

Joshua turned to the Tabernacle and altar of sacrifice.

"Henceforth shall Shiloh be the dwelling place of the Tabernacle and the ark of the covenant, and on festival days all Israel shall gather here to worship God," he said.

"As you say, so shall we do," the people answered.

"God has given you a land to inherit, and you have fought

for it and won it," Joshua said. "But you have not won it alone. God was with you, to let you win. Give thanks to God all the days of your life."

The people answered with one voice. "God is first, God is last, and there is no god beside God," they said.

"Go now to your tents in the land of your inheritance, and build altars of your own," Joshua said. Then he blessed the people and sent them on their way.

·22·
SHECHEM

Joshua had yet to fulfill Moses' command to bury the bones of Joseph in Shechem. As his time to die drew near, he prepared for it. And he prepared also to rededicate the people to God, for in the past they had fallen away from worshiping God, and he feared they might do so again after he was dead.

He sent word to the twelve tribes, now scattered throughout the land, to meet him in Shechem, and each tribe went out from its own land to journey there.

Joshua set up his tent on the parcel of land that Jacob had bought, near the great oak tree. And when the people were assembled and stood before him, he rose up under the oak tree and spoke to them.

"Hear, O Israel, we have but one God and one God alone," he said.

"Blessed and eternal is our God," the people answered.

Joshua turned toward his son. "Amram," he said, "place a stone under the tree, that it might be a witness to our words."

Amram, with the help of some others, rolled over a stone, and Joshua wrote on it the words of the Law that God had given on Mount Sinai.

"These are commandments that God has given you to obey," Joshua said. "And these words has God given me to speak to you. Heed the law of Moses. Do not worship other gods or mix with heathen nations. Cleave to me as you have done unto this day, and bind yourselves to me all the days of your lives."

"Our God is a great and a good God," the people answered. "God alone will we serve and to the voice of God will we hearken."

"The stone is a witness. You have heard God's words and promised to cleave to God," Joshua said.

Joshua then asked for a hole to be dug in the parcel of land that Jacob, Joseph's father, had bought, and in the presence of all, Joshua buried the bones of Joseph in it. Eleazar threw earth over the bones, sealing Joseph in the same earth where his parents also slept, in Hebron, in the south.

Joshua returned to the hilly lands of the north that had been given to his people, the tribe of Ephraim. He died when he was one hundred and ten years old and was buried in Timnath-serah, in the hills.

This has been Joshua's story. All that God had commanded Moses, so did Moses command Joshua, and so had Joshua done.

AFTERWORD

Joshua's fears came true. As each tribe settled in its own land and went its own way, the nation became divided. Their neighbors still worshiped idols. And with no strong leader to unite them or keep them faithful to God, the Israelites began to worship idols again.

The Philistines, a people living along the coast (Canaan was renamed Palestine because of them), conquered the land and overran it. They oppressed the Israelites and made it impossible for them to fight back by prohibiting blacksmiths to make tools and armor-makers to forge weapons for them. The Philistines destroyed the last thread that held some people together, the religious capital at Shiloh.

Then Samuel, a prophet, arose. He spoke to the people about God, about the promises their parents had made to God, and about the Law of Moses that had bound them together as a nation. He told them that in unity there was strength.

Samuel trained a group of young men to go about the land and speak to the people. With song and music, the young prophets sought to persuade Israel to return to God. They spoke of God's power and promised the people that if they returned to the worship of God, God would deliver them from their tormentors, just as He had delivered their ancestors from the Egyptians.

The Israelites once more became united. Now they wanted a king, like other nations, and Saul, of the tribe of Benjamin, was chosen king. He made the people bold again. His successor, King David, whose rule initiated the glorious and united kingdom of Israel, drove the Philistines out of the land and out to sea.

One hundred and fifty years after Joshua inherited the thirty-one cities, King David fought for and won the remainder of the Promised Land and made Jerusalem its capital.

But the land was invaded again and again. The Israelites, also called Hebrews or Jews, fled or were exiled from the land as conquerors from Babylon, Persia, Greece, and Rome came to possess it. In 70 c.e. (Common Era), Rome destroyed Jerusalem, ending the thousand-year existence of the Hebrew nation on its soil. The Romans killed the Jews, sold them into slavery, and drove them out of the land, whose name they had changed to Palestine. Islam conquered Palestine next, then Turkey. Individual Jews remained and returned in small numbers, living in the four holy cities—Jerusalem, Safad, Hebron, and Tiberias.

Following World War I, Turkey lost control of Palestine. The country was given by the League of Nations to Great Britain, with a mandate to establish there a homeland for the Jews. But Great Britain failed to do this, and the Jews began an underground battle against the British in a fight for liberation.

After six million European Jews were killed by Hitler in

World War II, the United Nations in 1947 repeated the aims of the League of Nations and gave a part of the land to be a homeland for the Jews.

The neighboring Arab countries rejected the idea of a Jewish state in their midst. In 1948, Lebanon, Syria, Trans-Jordan, Egypt, and Iraq invaded Palestine and made war against the Jews.

The Jews fought back. Some three thousand years after Joshua, they again found it necessary to "inherit" the land that had been promised them. They defeated their at-tackers, raised a flag over the land, and changed its name to Israel.